Birthday Celebrations

Written by Margie Burton, Cathy French, and Tammy Jones

My birthday is coming soon.
I am going to ask
my friends to come
to my birthday party.

I help my mother make my birthday cake. I am going to put in the milk.

5

6

Today is my birthday.
My mom and dad gave me
a shirt.

My friends are here for my party.

We will play games.

My birthday cake has six candles on it because I am six years old. I will make a wish when I blow them out. If I get them all, my wish will come true.

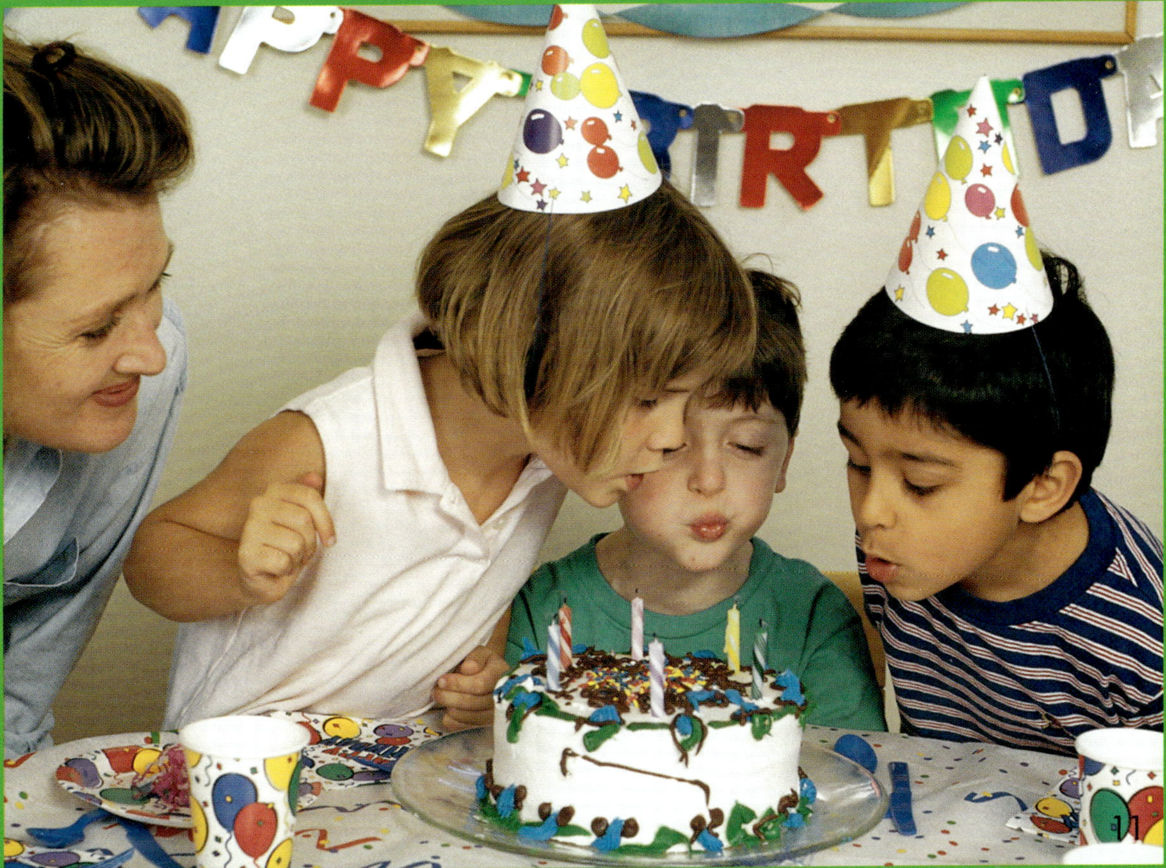

12

I like to open my presents.

We go outside
to blow bubbles.

15

My friends are going
to get a prize.